UFOs
and Other
Worlds

BY PETER RYAN

ILLUSTRATED BY

LUDEK PESEK

PUFFIN BOOKS

Explorer 17

for Lola and Martin

ACKNOWLEDGEMENTS

The author and publishers would like to thank the following for their
kind permission to include the photographs appearing in this book:

American Museum of Natural History, Hayden Planetarium, Art Work by
Helmut Wimmer: p. 21; Associated Press: p. 17; British Island
Airways: p. 8; Camera Préss: pp. 5, 7 and 33; Francis Greene: p. 9;
from Menzel, *A Field Guide to the Stars and Planets*, Houghton Mifflin
Company and Wm Collins: pp. 23 and 24; L.T.V. Aerospace Corporation: p. 7;
London Express News and Feature Services: p. 13; N.A.S.A.: pp. 7, 22, 45
and 46; Royal Astronomical Society, photograph from the Hale Observatories
p. 29 and Radcliffe Observatory p. 28; Syndication International Ltd: p. 40;
United States Air Force: p. 7.

Puffin Books: Penguin Books Ltd, Harmondsworth,
Middlesex, England
Penguin Books Inc., 7110 Ambassador Road,
Baltimore, Maryland 21207, U.S.A.
Penguin Books Australia Ltd, Ringwood,
Victoria, Australia
Penguin Books Canada Ltd,
41 Steelcase Road West, Markham, Ontario, Canada
Penguin Books (N.Z.) Ltd, 182–190 Wairau Road,
Auckland 10, New Zealand

First Published 1975
Text copyright © Peter Ryan, 1975
Colour illustrations copyright © Ludek Pesek, 1975

Made and printed in Great Britain by
Westerham Press Ltd, Westerham, Kent
Set in Monophoto Plantin

1947: The first 'flying saucers'.

The two words, *flying* and *saucer*, were first put together by an American journalist in a newspaper report in the summer of 1947. He used the phrase to describe nine shiny *unidentified flying objects*, or *UFOs* for short, which a civilian pilot had spotted from his aeroplane. The pilot had been searching for the wreck of another plane, which had crashed in the Rocky Mountains. He was flying between two peaks when he saw the objects beneath him. They seemed to him to be travelling at more than twice the speed of sound, and that was in the days before the sound barrier had been broken. When he landed and reported what he had seen, his story made the headlines.

Sometime later an investigation discovered that a formation of United States Airforce planes had been flying over the Rocky Mountains at about the same time that the civilian pilot saw the

UFOs. The flying saucers were almost certainly these planes glinting in the sunlight as they flew among the mountain ridges. This explanation was printed in the newspapers, but already the idea that America was being visited by mysterious flying machines had caught the public imagination and was fast gaining enormous popularity.

Reports about fiery airborne devices and lights in the sky have been around since ancient times. From time to time they receive a lot of publicity, and the summer of 1947 was one of these times. Everyone wanted to read about flying saucers. All kinds of books were written. People who liked to read ghost stories, fairy tales or accounts of vanishing ships now wanted to read about UFOs. Newspapers printed stories about visits to Earth by mysterious machines and strange creatures from outer space, but most of these stories were little more than science fiction, and only a few people took them seriously. Then, in 1952, the United States Airforce revealed that its pilots too had been seeing UFOs. The influential *Life* magazine, which was read by millions, published an article about flying saucers. Questions were asked. Were UFOs really from Planet X? If not, were they perhaps some terrible new secret weapon? The public wanted the answers and scientists were called in to provide them.

Unfortunately nothing upsets most scientists more than the subject of flying saucers. It even makes them get angry with each other. One expert will say that UFOs are indeed a mystery that we cannot yet understand, while another will say that this is rubbish and that all flying saucers will turn out to be quite ordinary objects and events when they are properly investigated.

Many scientists do not like to discuss UFOs in public. When the highly respected American Association for the Advancement of Science decided to hold a meeting on the subject several of its most distinguished members tried to have it cancelled, but eventually the meeting took place and for two days in Boston in 1969 some of the best brains in America pondered the problems of ufology (as the 'science' of UFOs is called). The main difficulty, these scientists agreed, was lack of good evidence. Scientists are like detectives. A scientist likes to take whatever he is studying into his laboratory. If this is not possible, he likes to go to where he can find the subject of his inquiries in its normal environment. He can study jungle trees by visiting the Amazon. He can study the effects of living in space by spending some time in orbit. Sometimes he must be content with a third method. He cannot, for example, carry the sun or the stars into his laboratory, nor can he hope to visit them; he can only observe them.

When it comes to investigating UFOs the scientist has a difficult time. No one has ever managed to lure a flying saucer into a laboratory. Indeed only a very few *trained* observers have ever seen UFOs. In many cases there is only just enough evidence to make them interesting. This is fine for a newspaper editor who simply has to report the mystery object or whatever it is, but very troublesome for the serious scientific investigator.

Often the little evidence that exists turns out to be most unreliable. One night in 1968 several citizens of a small community in Colorado called Castle Rock saw a UFO. A local newspaper reported their descriptions. One man said it was 'a large bubble-shaped object'. Another said he saw 'a dozen bright lights'. A third man said he had seen 'a single big bright light, at least twenty-five feet (7.6 m) in diameter'. While yet another described the egg-shaped bubble as 'about fifty feet (15.2 m) long, twenty feet (6.1 m) wide and twenty feet deep'. The scientists trying to investigate this particular flying saucer soon realized that they would have a hard time trying to decide which, if any, of these descriptions was accurate. In the event two boys saved them the trouble. The night the flying saucer was sighted they had set fire to a small plastic bag full of hydrogen and let it float up into the sky. This is what the surprised citizens had seen. They had greatly exaggerated its size.

A glowing gas bubble produced in a laboratory. How big would you say it is?

The answer is about one inch (2.5 cm). When it is dark, small bright objects appear to be much larger than they really are. The list below shows the variety of objects and events which have frequently caused people to think they have seen flying saucers.

balloons and blimps
beacon lights
birds
bubbles
cigarette ends
clouds
comets
dust storms
feathers
fireworks
flares
fog and mist reflections
insect swarms
kites
leaves
lighthouses
lightning
meteors
military experiments
the moon
parachutes

planes, especially experimental aircraft or aircraft reflecting the light of the sun or the moon; their navigation or landing lights
planets
rockets
satellites passing overhead or burning up when re-entering the earth's atmosphere
searchlight reflections from low cloud
smoke
spider webs
stars
street lamps
the sun
tumbleweed
vapour trails
window reflections

This list is far from complete. All kinds of everyday objects and events can result in a UFO story. In France one autumn night a report spread through a village that the Martians had landed. Women and children were herded into the safety of the local church while the men armed themselves and set out to investigate. Advancing upon the 'landing site', they shone their torches at the 'intruders'. The short figures with large white heads stood silently before them. The men were about to charge when they realized their mistake. The 'Martians' were nothing more than large chrysanthemum plants covered with white cloths to protect them from the frost.

There are not enough scientists interested in flying saucers to ensure that every single UFO report is investigated, but every now and again events take place which are so mysterious and tantalizing that even the busiest of UFO experts will drop everything and take

UFOs? No. They are:
1 unusual saucer-shaped clouds photographed in Brazil.
2 a typical meteor.
3 a smoke ring from an experimental explosion which was mistaken for a flying saucer.
4 an experimental plane called a 'flying pancake', which could be mistaken for a flying saucer when seen from below.

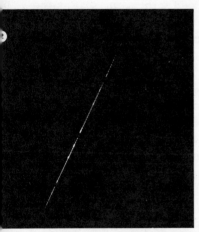

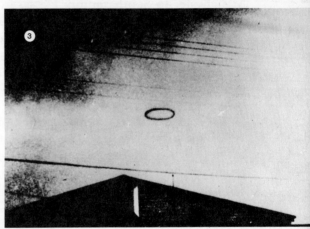

up the challenge. This happened in England in 1966. On a flight from Manchester to Southampton one summer morning a woman passenger was looking out of the aeroplane window when she saw what looked like another plane following close behind. It was a curious cigar-shaped craft with fins at either end. Her husband who was sitting next to her had a cine camera on his lap. She picked up the camera and filmed the finned object through the aeroplane window. The film was developed and was later shown on television. A scientist who was interested in flying saucers saw the film. He was a little sceptical and decided to try an experiment. Taking a cine camera with him, he went for a ride on the same plane on the same flight from Manchester to Southampton. He sat in exactly the same seat as the woman and he too saw the UFO. Some frames from the film he made are shown on the right. Thanks to this scientist, the UFO became an *IFO*, or *identified flying object*. It was nothing stranger than the tip of the aeroplane in which he was flying seen through the curved edge of one of the plane's windows. Aircraft windows have curved edges to make them strong. You can see the same effects for yourself by looking at the world through an empty milk bottle.

Curved glass provides us with the occasional good flying saucer mystery. It also enables a lot of people with bad eyesight to see better, as anyone who has to wear spectacles knows. Such people can easily imagine they see odd things when they take their spectacles off.

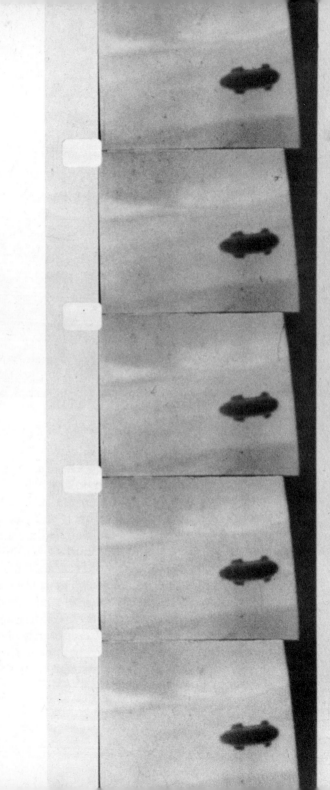

The 1966 UFO film (right),
and (left) the British Island
Airways Dart Herald from which
it was taken. Notice especially
the tips of the tail fins.

The missionary's UFO.

A few minutes after sunset one evening in the summer of 1959, a missionary on the island of New Guinea was gazing up into the sky. It had just stopped raining, when he saw a large U F O flitting in and out of some low clouds. Standing on the deck of the saucer-shaped craft he saw several man-like creatures, and he waved to them. To his surprise they waved back. He watched for a few minutes more, but the craft vanished behind the clouds. Everyone the priest told his tale to believed him, but no one could explain it to him.

Several years later an American astronomer was looking up at the evening star, the planet Venus. He had heard of the missionary's experiences and he decided to try an experiment. Using a special pair of spectacles he made himself temporarily short-sighted. The lenses he used also made round objects appear to be flattened. When he looked up at the planet Venus through these spectacles it seemed to be fuzzy and saucer-shaped, very like the flying saucer the missionary

had described. From this part of his experiment, the astronomer deduced that the missionary was probably naturally short-sighted, and that he suffered from astigmatism, which is the scientific name for a sight defect which causes round objects to appear flattened.

When not wearing a pair of spectacles, a naturally short-sighted person may often close his or her eyes slightly in an attempt to see things more clearly. So, for the second part of his experiment, the astronomer did just that. Looking at the fuzzy planet he now saw some thread-like shapes which, with a bit of imagination, could have been mistaken for man-like figures. As the astronomer blinked, these thread-like shapes moved, but they were not man-like creatures from outer space, they were the astronomer's own eyelashes. Unfortunately the astronomer did not manage to find the missionary and test his eyesight, but few people still doubt the results of his very clever detective work.

There are times when even persons with perfect eyesight can be tricked into seeing something which is not really there. If you look at the picture below it seems to be a spiral, but if you look at it more carefully you will see that it is not. It is a series of circles, one inside the other. Pictures like this, which deceive the eye, produce what is called an optical illusion. Flying saucers may sometimes turn out to be illusions. If the eye can sometimes deceive, so can the brain. For example, when you dream you can 'see', 'hear', 'touch' and even 'taste' and 'smell' all kinds of objects which are not real. Some people can be made to 'see' unreal things when they are under the influence of various drugs. All these situations can produce flying saucer stories. People may sometimes believe they have seen something which is not really there.

The object the policemen are looking at is real enough. It is one of six similar objects which were found at various points along a straight line stretching from Somerset to Kent, one morning in the summer of 1967. The Army, the Air Force, police and scientists were all alerted when reports began to come in from a postman, a golfer and a newsboy on his paper round. Each of them had stumbled upon a shiny metallic saucer-shaped object emitting strange bleeping sounds. As the morning went on there were reports of lights in the sky and odd noises the night before. By the time the sixth object had been found, the excitement was enormous. A whole squadron of UFOs, it seemed, had landed in England. Now at last there was something real for the scientists to examine. The first saucer was opened up and there inside was . . . an ordinary second-hand tape recorder, the property of some clever hoaxers from a technical college.

If you saw a U F O in the sky and you did not know whether it was really there or whether you were just seeing things, one way of finding out would be to use a radar set. A radar set uses radar waves instead of light waves to see things. When you shine a torch at something in the dark, you are sending out light waves. These light waves bounce off the objects around you and return to your eyes so that you can see the objects. A radar set sends out radar waves. They also bounce off objects and when these radar waves return to the set you can see the objects on a screen. An object the size of an aeroplane would appear as a dot or 'blip'. Of course not many people have a radar set to hand but most aeroplanes particularly those of the United States Airforce (U S A F) are equipped with them.

One night in 1957 a U S A F plane was flying inland across the Gulf of Mexico. When it reached the coast of the State of Mississippi, one of the radar operators on board saw a blip on his radar screen. An object seemed to be following the plane. A few minutes later the pilot looked out of his cockpit window and saw what he thought to be the landing lights of another plane flying towards him. The co-pilot also

An artist's impression of the USAF pilots' UFO, which also showed up on their radar screen.

saw the lights, but they both noticed the red, white or green navigation lights, which planes normally show at night, were not to be seen. They were thinking how unusual this was when the bright lights flashed past them and disappeared. The radar screen showed that the object was now flying in front of them. By this time they were approaching the USAF base at Duncanville in Texas, so the pilot called up the base on his radio and asked them to check whether they could see anything unusual on their radar screens. The base confirmed that there was indeed an unidentified object flying along ahead of them. The plane followed the object and from time to time the pilots could see a bright light, but when they tried to close in on it the light vanished. They kept up the chase until their fuel supply indicator told them it was time to land.

Sometime later the USAF investigation team which was trying to solve this puzzling mystery discovered that two civilian airliners nearly collided over Texas on that same night. This, they suggested, might explain the presence of the unusual lights and radar blips. It was not a very good explanation and it caused some people to say that the USAF was not telling the whole story, this UFO sighting will probably remain a mystery forever.

Almost every day somebody somewhere in the world sees something strange in the sky. In 1965 several thousand Americans were asked if they had ever seen an airborne object which they could not identify. From their answers it has been calculated that as many as five million Americans have some experience of UFOs. We get to hear about the more spectacular flying saucers from radio, television and newspaper reports, but these are only a tiny percentage of the total number of UFO events. Reports of flying saucers come from all parts of the world and they are collected by various organizations. The United States Airforce has records of more than twelve thousand UFO sightings. In America reports are also collected by the National Investigations Committee on Aerial Phenomena (NICAP) set up by the Government in 1956, and the Aerial Phenomena Research Organization (APRO) founded in 1952. In England there is the British Unidentified Flying Object Research Association (BUFORA) set up in 1962, and the Unidentified Flying Object Investigation Society (UFOIS) which was founded in 1963. There are similar organizations in France, Belgium, Denmark, Finland, Germany, Holland, Italy, Japan, Spain, Australia and New Zealand. The number of UFO reports varies from year to year, but since 1947 the USAF has kept records of sightings in the USA. Here is a list from these records.

Year	Number of sightings or events reported	Year	Number of sightings or events reported
1947	122	1959	390
1948	156	1960	557
1949	186	1961	591
1950	210	1962	474
1951	169	1963	399
1952	1,501	1964	562
1953	509	1965	887
1954	487	1966	1,112
1955	545	1967	937
1956	690	1968	375
1957	1,006	1969	146
1958	627		

1952, 1957 and 1966 are years in which there were more than one thousand reports of UFO sightings or events. Some people will tell you that this is the result of planned UFO 'invasions', but there is a

New York before ... and after the power failure of 9 November 1965. Power was restored after 10 hours.

simpler explanation. 1952 was the year the USAF first revealed that its pilots were sometimes seeing UFOs. That launched the biggest UFO scare in American history. It was kept rolling by *Life* magazine which published a big flying saucer report. 1957 was the year of Sputnik, the first artificial satellite to be put into orbit. The score for 1966 is explained by events which took place one night in November 1965 when a power failure blacked out New York City.

In the early autumn of 1965 more than seventy reports were recorded from the north-eastern part of the United States telling of

An artist's impression of the Kentucky glowing man. ▶

large bright bubble-shaped UFOs hovering near high power electric transmission lines. Some people suggested that these were flying saucers recharging their batteries. Then came the power failure which blacked out New York and plunged the city into chaos. The UFOs, it was suggested, had blown the fuses! It took the men in charge of the power network some time to restore the supply and to work out what had happened. Then it was found that an important switch had been accidentally turned off. It was not the work of UFOs, but an ordinary human error. As for the flying saucers seen hovering near the power lines, it appears they were quite natural clouds of glowing gas which gather round high-power electrical equipment in certain unusual weather conditions. But the power blackout brought UFOs back into the news, and the following year, 1966, was another bumper year for flying saucer reports. When flying saucers make the headlines, the number of people on the look-out for them increases. One UFO, it seems, leads to another.

Ninety-five per cent of the UFO reports from the files of the United States Airforce have been explained; but this leaves a few hundred which are still unsolved. In some of these cases there is not enough evidence to go on, in others the stories of the witnesses are so extraordinary that nobody has been able to think up an explanation.

One of these unexplained stories is the tale of the Kentucky Glowing Man. Late one evening in 1955 a farmer was standing outside his farmhouse in a remote part of Kentucky when he saw a flying saucer land behind some trees. He went inside and told his family. Nobody would believe his story. An hour later the family were alerted by one of their dogs which was barking angrily. Two men went outside to investigate and they found what they later described as 'a small glowing man with large red eyes' walking towards the house. This strange sight scared the farmers, but as they were carrying rifles they began to shoot at their luminous intruder. A metallic sound told them that they had hit their target and they stopped firing, but the glowing man seemed unharmed and simply 'floated away into some trees'. The two men went back into the house and bolted all the doors. A few moments later the glowing man peered in through one of the farmhouse windows. The two farmers rushed outside to chase him off, but their visitor had vanished. They searched all round the outbuildings, and suddenly one of the men felt a tap on his head. He looked up and saw a claw-like hand reaching down towards him from a low roof.

The men fled back to the house, packed the family into two cars, and drove off to the local police station to seek help. The police went up to the farm but, in spite of a very thorough search, they could find no trace of the unwelcome guest. The story remains a complete and baffling mystery. What do you think? Was it a hoax?

When someone asks the question: 'Do you believe in flying saucers?', you may say 'No' because you think that all UFOs will turn out to be ordinary objects or events if you have enough evidence for your detective work, or you may say 'Yes' because you like to think that at least some flying saucers are interplanetary or interstellar spaceships from another world. The third answer is always: 'I don't know' because there will always be unanswered questions. It is rather disappointing that there is no good scientific evidence that flying saucers piloted by intelligent creatures who live elsewhere in space visit our planet, but this is no reason why we should stop wondering whether there are such creatures living on other planets in the universe.

The Solar System and the Milky Way by Helmut Wimmer.

When we look at our home planet from outer space, we see that it is one of a family of nine. Ours is the third one from the centre, and when we look closely at photographs of its surface taken by spacecraft, we can see plenty of signs of life upon it.

Spacecraft have also provided us with photographs of the surfaces of some of the other planets of our sun. Looking through his telescope, the American astronomer Percival Lowell thought he saw canals on Mars. He believed that these canals had been dug by Martians. That was in 1895. In 1972 the American spacecraft Mariner 9 took the photograph shown below. What it shows is not a canal. It appears to be a dried up river course. There are no signs of Martians or any other kind of life, but this valley is still a mystery because we do not think there is any water on Mars today.

Venus and Mercury cannot be inhabited because they are too hot for life as we know it. The five planets beyond Mars are almost certainly too cold.

A Martian valley photographed by an American interplanetary spacecraft.

Alpha Centauri.

We must look outside our solar system for intelligent neighbours, if such neighbours exist. The view from a spacecraft travelling between the planets reminds us that our sun is just one of the many millions of stars which make up a vast family of stars called the Milky Way. In turn the Milky Way is one of many millions of star families we call galaxies.

Not all of these stars are like our sun. Some are many thousands of times bigger, others are much smaller. Many stars exist in pairs and even threesomes. These twins and triplets circle around each other slowly. There are also other planets, but we cannot hope to see them, even with our most powerful telescopes, because they are so far away.

We measure the distances between stars in light years. Light travels very fast, about 187,500 miles (300,000 km) every second. So a light year is a long way, about 5,875,000,000,000 miles (9,400,000,000,000 km). The sun's closest neighbouring star is a set of triplets called Alpha Centauri.

In the photograph above, two of the Alpha Centauri triplets are shown. The third is too faint to be seen clearly. These three stars

(above) *Sirius,* (below) *The Milky Way Galaxy.*

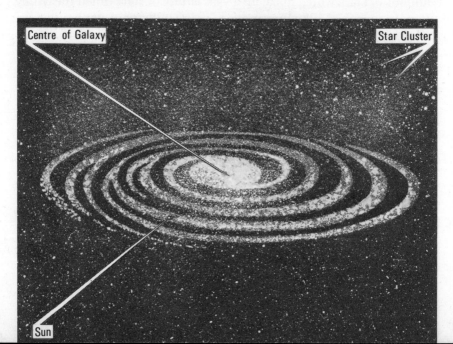

are about 4.2 light years away. Using the rockets we have today, a journey to Alpha Centauri would take thousands of years. In our part of the Milky Way interstellar astronauts would have to live lives much longer than the present human life-span to make such journeys worth while, unless spaceships could be constructed which would travel faster than light; but according to our present state of scientific knowledge, that is impossible.

To get a really good view of Alpha Centauri you need to be south of the equator, but if you live in the Northern Hemisphere you can see one of our sun's other close neighbours, Sirius, the brightest star in the sky.

Sirius is located 8.6 light years away. It has a comparatively tiny twin. This twin is a type of star called a white dwarf. Though they are quite small as stars go, white dwarves are very heavy. The matter from which they are made is highly compressed. A teaspoonful of the matter which makes up the white dwarf twin of Sirius would weigh about a ton (1.016 tonne).

If there are planets orbiting the suns of Alpha Centauri or Sirius with its attendant partners, their inhabitants, if such creatures exist, would be accustomed to living with more than one sun in the sky. This would also mean that they would be used to having more than one shadow.

The stars of our Milky Way galaxy form a gigantic spiral with a diameter of about 100,000 light years. In the centre of this spiral, some 30,000 light years away from us, the stars are quite close together like houses in the centre of a city. Our sun and its neighbours live in a suburb of this centre, where the stars are farther apart, like houses in the country. Away from the centre there are also clusters of closely spaced stars like small towns away from the capital city. The photograph on the left shows one of these star clusters in our galaxy. It lies about 20,000 light years away from us. The suns of these star clusters are probably only separated by a few light months. At night any inhabitants of their planets would have a spectacular view of the heavens about them.

Galaxies are the building blocks of the universe. Our Milky Way galaxy is one of a group of twenty-seven galaxies. The Andromeda Spiral is another member of this group, and is the most distant object we can see in the night sky with the naked eye. It is about 2.2 million

25

An artist's impression of the surface of a planet with two suns. ▶
One of the suns is a white dwarf; its twin is a large red star.

A typical star cluster.

light years away. The light we see from Andromeda left that galaxy when our ancient ape-like ancestors were fashioning their pebble tools on river banks and lake shores. The light from the most distant galaxies that we can see through a telescope has been travelling across space since the time of the birth of our planet some 5,000 million years ago.

Other groups contain thousands of galaxies. The total number of galaxies in the universe is measured in millions. If we begin to add up the total number of stars in the heavens, we soon lose count, so if you are looking for planets, there are plenty of places to look.

If we were able to build impossibly fast spaceships, there would not be much point in setting off in search of other inhabited worlds unless we knew where to look. Trying to decide which of the nearer stars might have planets suitable for the evolution of life is not easy. We cannot see other inhabited planetary systems in our galaxy, but we can try *listening* for signs of them.

28

The spiral galaxy of Andromeda

(overleaf) *On its journey beyond our Solar System
a spacecraft passes the planet Pluto*

Astronomers use enormous radio telescopes like the one at Jodrell Bank in Cheshire to listen to the stars. Many of the stars we can see with our optical telescopes send us not only light waves, but also transmit radio waves. These transmissions are caused quite naturally by physical events going on in and around the fiery matter from which stars are made. When we listen to these interstellar radio signals, they do not, at first, seem very exciting. They sound rather like an egg being fried in hot fat, but from this crackling sound an astronomer can build up a radio 'picture' of the star he is listening to.

If a radio astronomer from a planet circling a nearby star happened to be listening to our solar system, he would hear the sun and possibly the giant planet Jupiter which also transmits radio signals.

If his radio telescope were very big indeed, he might also detect a confused mixture of radio, television and radar signals produced by man. He would then begin to realize that he had found an inhabited planet. By watching and listening he might learn quite a lot about us, but whether he would think that we were worth visiting is difficult to decide.

Looking for extraterrestrial civilizations, as other planets inhabited by intelligent creatures are sometimes called, has already been tried. Using a comparatively small radio telescope in Virginia, an American astronomer called Frank Drake tuned into some of the sun's closer neighbours in 1960. He was hoping to eavesdrop on some cosmic conversation, but he heard nothing. Then in the summer of 1964 the Russian newspapers and radio announced that a group of Soviet astronomers had received some signals from outer space which were thought to be the result of the activities of 'extraterrestrial intelligences'. A few years later a team of astronomers at Cambridge University in England received similar signals, but they chose to keep quiet about their 'little green men' as they called them. It turned out that these signals had a natural origin. They are produced by stars called pulsars whose radio transmissions are more complicated than those from ordinary stars. It was the first time they had been heard, so it was natural that they should cause a lot of excitement.

The radio telescopes we have today are probably not sensitive enough for listening to radio transmissions from other civilizations. By the time their signals had crossed the enormous distances between

Two men stand in the giant electronic ear of the Jodrell Bank radio telescope in Cheshire, England.

stars, they would be too weak for our receivers to detect. We would have a better chance of hearing something if the inhabitants of these civilizations were using very powerful transmitters designed to send messages across interstellar distances. They might be doing this for two reasons. The first is that two or more civilizations might already be in touch with each other by radio. They would need powerful transmitters to hear each other. The second reason is that the inhabitants of another world might be using such transmitters to draw attention to themselves, to inform other inhabited worlds of their existence.

If we ever do receive a radio signal from another world, we can hardly expect it to be in English, or any other Earth language for that matter. The inhabitants of a remote planet could not be expected to know our alphabets.

33

An artist's impression of the surface of a planet orbiting a sun within a star cluster. ▶

The simplest of all radio alphabets consists of dots and dashes. Let us imagine that a radio astronomer was scanning the sky one day when he began to pick up a simple message: dash, dot, dash, dot, dot, dot, dash, dot, dash, then a pause, and the message is repeated over and over.

— • — • • • — • —

At first the astronomer would be mystified. The morse code we use has no letters with a mixture of nine dots and dashes, but the number nine is a clue. Nine is three times three. There is no other way of dividing nine into whole numbers. Let us see what happens if we arrange the nine dots and dashes into a three by three square.

— • —
• • •
— • —

Take away the dashes and we have a simple picture of a star.

•
• • •
•

A longer message might have twenty five dots and dashes.

— — • — • • • • • — — • — — — • — • — — • — • —

Enough for a square measuring five by five.

— — • — —
• • • • •
— — • — —
— • — • —
— • — • —

Take away the dashes:

•
• • • • •
•
• •
• •

Now we have a figure with two legs, two arms, but not much of a head.

Here is a message made up of 361 dots and dashes. 361 is nineteen times nineteen. There is no other way we can divide 361 into whole numbers. The message begins:

— — • • • — — — — — — — — — — — — — • — — — • — — — — — —
— — — — — • — • — — — — • — — — — — — — — —

and so on. Here is the complete message arranged as a nineteen by nineteen square:

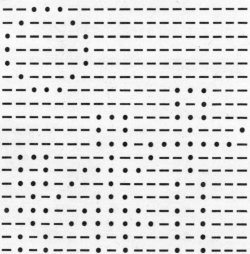

Take away the dashes:

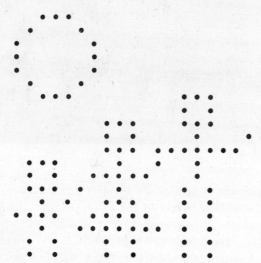

There are three figures holding hands. On the left is a child. In the middle is his or her mother and on the right is his or her father. There is a single sun behind them. It is worth mentioning that if the astronomer who received this message was Arabic, or Chinese, he

Project Cyclops. The proposed orchard of electronic ears.

would not begin his square at the top left hand corner. However he would still get a mirror image of the same picture. There is another message on page 46. It has not yet been arranged into a square. You might like to find a piece of graph paper and try and decode it.

The largest dish-shaped radio telescopes we have in use today have diameters of about 325 feet (100 m). These dishes weigh thousands of tonnes. We could build larger dishes, but they would weigh so much that they would be difficult to control, so one way round this problem is to use more than one dish.

Such a project was proposed in a report published in 1972 by an American scientist called Bernard Oliver. He suggested the construction of an orchard of electronic ears. All working together they would have the same sensitivity as a dish with a diameter measured in miles or kilometres. Project Cyclops, as this proposal is called, would enable us to listen in to many thousands of stars in the hope of making contact by radio with another world.

Because of the daunting size of the universe, we would be sensible to restrict our search for extraterrestrial civilizations to our own Milky

The Mekon, 'arch-criminal of the Solar System, was once again established on his home planet Venus...' Dan Dare's old enemy from the pages of the comic Eagle, and one of the most famous fictional 'intelligent beings'. Notice particularly his large head and small limbs.

O MASTER, DAN DARE AND THE EARTHLINGS FROM THE *MAGENTA* HAVE SURVIVED. NOW THAT THE AUTHORITIES KNOW THAT YOU ARE ON VENUS, THEY WILL BE WATCHFUL!

THEN WE SHALL ATTACK BEFORE THEY CAN PREPARE FOR US! NOTHING CAN STOP OUR PLAN - NOT EVEN DAN DARE

Way galaxy. It contains millions of stars like our sun which provide the light and warmth needed for the evolution of life. We do not yet know how many of these stars have planets circling around them at distances where they are neither scorched like Mercury nor left out in the cold like the frozen world of Pluto. We do know that our planet was born out of a blob of molten matter some 5,000 million years ago, and that by about 3,500 million years ago the rain began to fall and the planet began to cool down. Soon after that the chemistry of life began. So we can say that it has taken about 3,500 million years for man to evolve on this planet. Now we are wondering if the same process has taken place elsewhere in our galaxy.

Astronomers reckon the Milky Way galaxy is about 12,000 million years old. We do not think that all the planets in our galaxy will be the same age. If the process of evolution is taking place on other planets, it might be happening more quickly or more slowly than it does on earth. This means that, if there are other inhabited worlds, some will still be at the equivalent of the dinosaur stage, while others will be far in advance of our civilization. These advanced civilizations would be very interesting to discover. Their inhabitants might live in what we would think of as a science-fiction world, with all kinds of mysterious powers and knowledge.

It is an amusing pastime to try and imagine what intelligent creatures of another world might look like. All the advanced life forms on earth are made out of cells. These tiny living factories are joined together to make up all plants and animals. Most animals have holes at one end to take in air, water and food, and holes at the other end to get rid of waste products. At the end which takes in air, water and food there are also parts of the body which can see, hear, touch, smell and taste. Most animals have some way of moving around. The whole design is very practical for living on our planet and it is quite reasonable to suppose that the same basic formula has been evolved on other worlds. You might like to think up some improvements. For example, intelligence on earth depends on having a brain. If you want to spend your life thinking, and doing nothing else, you might not need various other parts of your body.

If we do find another inhabited world by using a system like Project Cyclops, we will have great difficulty keeping in touch. Our earth-bound radio receiver will revolve with the surface of the rotating

A listening ear in space. ▶

earth, so we will only be able to listen or send messages for half a day at a time. We could solve this problem by constructing a large receiving and transmitting station in space where contact could be kept up twenty-four hours a day.

When the first transatlantic telephone cable connected telephone users in London with those in New York 4,000 miles away across the ocean, a famous Englishman called Oscar Wilde was asked what he thought of this magnificent piece of engineering: 'It depends, Sir, on what they have to say,' was his reply. This would also be true of the value of interstellar communication.

Some people have even suggested that, if we did receive a message from another world, we should not reply. These people think it would be risky to reveal ourselves to the rest of the universe. They fear an invasion from outer space by creatures who might see us as a hopelessly primitive life-form to be kept as amusing pets, or, still worse, they might carry humans away to their home planet to serve up to their friends as exotic tasty delicacies. On our planet, contact between two races of men with different ways of life has almost always resulted in the domination of the weaker by the stronger. This is a very pessimistic suggestion and is the result of judging unknown intelligent beings by our own deplorable standards. Anyway it is too late. A message has already been sent.

The picture opposite is at this moment speeding away from our solar system towards the stars. It is fixed to a spacecraft called Pioneer 10 which sent us the photograph of Jupiter shown on page 46. It shows a man and a woman drawn to the same scale as the spacecraft. Below the figures are the planets with a line to show that the space-craft came from the third one which is earth and flew past the fifth one which is Jupiter. The star-like object is a radio map of our sun's position in this part of the galaxy.

Pioneer 10 is at present cruising through interstellar space at speeds measured in thousands, not millions, of kilometres an hour. This means that it will not reach another solar system in the fore-seeable future, but another way in which we have advertised our presence is a result of our use of high-powered radio, television and radar transmitters within the last thirty or so years. Some of their signals have passed, either intentionally or unintentionally, through the earth's atmosphere and are today still radiating out into space, like the ripples from a stone thrown into a pond, at the speed of light. Early radar signals, like those which were used by the Royal Air Force to detect enemy planes during the Second World War, have by now reached perhaps a hundred of the sun's neighbouring stars, but like the ripples from the splash in the pond they become weaker and weaker as they travel away from the centre. It is almost certain that it would be impossible to detect them today, unless someone was looking for them with an unimaginably sensitive receiver. The more powerful the signal, the better the chance of its being picked up, if there is anyone listening. Radio and television programmes are normally radiated from transmitters in all directions, but it is also possible to concentrate the power of some transmitters to send a strong signal along a beam. America's space organization, NASA, uses this type of transmission to keep in touch with its spacecraft.

The plaque attached to the American spacecraft Pioneer 10.

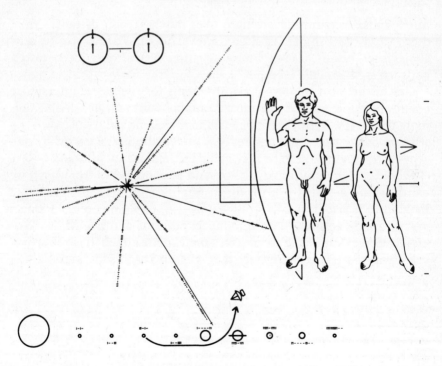

Such signals retain their strength over much greater distances than those from radiating transmitters. Powerful signals can also be sent along laser beams. Laser communication has already been tested between earth and the moon.

One of the most important requirements for successful interstellar communication will be patience. Contacts with another civilization more than a few light years away will involve long delays between the sending of messages and any reply. Conversations started off by one generation might have to be kept going by their grandchildren.

One day, ten, a hundred, a thousand or more years from now, we can imagine a starship cruising in our part of the galaxy when a lookout calls attention to a strange unidentified flying object. Pioneer 10 has made contact. The starship experts of another Milky Way civilization examine the picture on a metal plate attached to the spacecraft from planet earth. Perhaps they will send us this message:

```
--------------------------•••••••••-----------•--------•-----
-----•--------•--------•--------•----•--------•--------•-----
-----•----•--------•--------•--------•--------•--------•-----
-----•••••••••----•--------•--------•---•--------•----•---
--•--------•-•--------•---•--------•---•--------•-•--------•--
---•----•----•----•--------•-•--------•-•--------•--------•-----
--------------------•--------
```

46

Index